Writing Garden

Student book

1

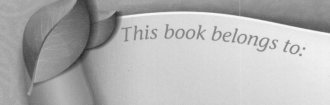

This book belongs to:

How to Use Writing Garden

Writing Sprouts

A. Story

Students talk about the pictures and try to guess what the story is about. They also learn the key vocabulary with the help of the pictures.

B. Questions with the Graphic Organizer

This comprehension activity will help the students to better understand the story. Students also learn how the ideas are developed and organized with the help of the graphic organizer.

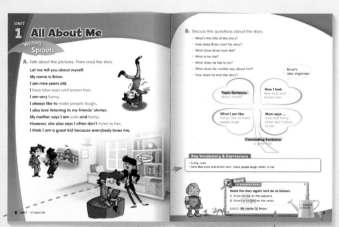

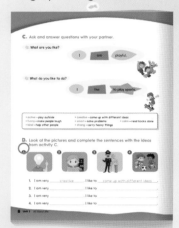

Key Vocabulary & Expressions

Students learn the key vocabulary and expressions.

Hunt for Sentence Parts

Students learn sentence structure by identifying the subject and verb in a sentence.

C. Speaking Activity

Students work with partners, and ask and answer questions related to the topic. This speaking activity will help the students to practice making sentences, and it will reinforce the acquisition of some of the many different expressions in English. Words and expressions are provided to guide the students.

D. Details

This activity will help the students to produce more ideas for their own story.

Workbook

Sentence Practice

Students put the words in order and learn correct sentence structure.

Writing Process

🐝 Planning

Students brainstorm their ideas with the teacher and write them in the blanks. Students are encouraged to write any ideas that come to mind. Word Bank is available to guide the students.

🐝 Adding Your Own Ideas

Depending on the level of the students, they can either complete the given topic sentence and concluding sentence, or write their own sentences in the blank lines. This activity helps the students to learn the correct choice of words and useful phrases to express ideas.

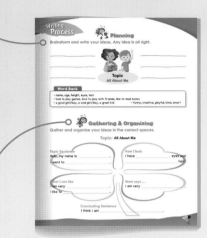

🐝 Gathering & Organizing

Students develop and organize their own ideas from the planning stage. The idea organizer will guide the students in writing their ideas in a more organized way.

🐝 My 1ˢᵗ Draft

Through the activity of rewriting the story, students can learn how the writing is utilized and developed in a paragraph. Students peer check their writing using the checklist at the bottom of the page. This will help the students to learn correct sentence structure.

🍃 Revising Practice

Students find any mistakes in the story and correct them. Students expand the sentences with the given words. This activity will help the students learn how to revise their writing and learn how to write longer sentences.

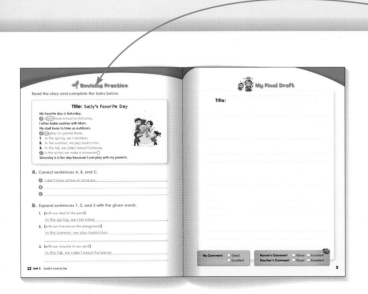

🐝 My Final Draft

Students make sure there are no mistakes in their final draft. Students can experience and understand the entire writing process by going through the exercises given from the first step (Planning) to the last step (My Final Draft).

Contents

Example: Danny plants flowers.

V (verb)

S (subject)

S (subject)
V (verb)

Danny plants flowers.
S: Who plants flowers? Danny.
V: What does Danny do? He plants flowers.

All About Me

Writing Sprouts

A. Talk about the pictures. Then read the story.

Let me tell you about myself.

My name is Brian.

I am nine years old.

I have blue eyes and brown hair.

I am very funny.

I always like to make people laugh.

I also love listening to my friends' stories.

My mother says I am cute and funny.

However, she also says I often don't listen to her.

I think I am a great kid because everybody loves me.

B. Discuss the questions about the story.

- What's the title of the story?
- How does Brian start his story?
- What does Brian look like?
- What is he like?
- What does he like to do?
- What does his mother say about him?
- How does he end the story?

Brian's idea organizer

Topic Sentence
about myself

How I look
blue eyes and
brown hair

What I am like
funny, like to make
people laugh

Mom says ...
cute and funny,
often don't listen
to her

Concluding Sentence
a great kid

Key Vocabulary & Expressions

- funny, cute
- have blue eyes and brown hair, make people laugh, listen to her

Hunt for Sentence Parts

Read the story again and do as follows:

1. Draw circles on the subjects.
2. Draw rectangles on the verbs.

Example My name is Brian.

Subject S
Verb V

C. Ask and answer questions with your partner.

Q: What are you like?

I   am   playful.

Q: What do you like to do?

I   like   to play sports.

- active—play outside
- funny—make people laugh
- kind—help other people
- creative—come up with different ideas
- smart—solve problems
- strong—carry heavy things
- calm—read books alone

D. Look at the pictures and complete the sentences with the ideas from activity C.

1    **2**    **3**    **4**

1. I am very _____creative_____. I like to _____come up with different ideas_____.

2. I am very _____. I like to _____.

3. I am very _____. I like to _____.

4. I am very _____. I like to _____.

Writing Process

 **Planning**

Brainstorm and write your ideas. Any idea is all right.

_____   _____

_____   _____

_____   _____

Topic
All About Me

Word Bank

- name, age, height, eyes, hair
- love to play games, love to play with friends, like to read books
- a good girl/boy, a cool girl/boy, a great kid   • funny, creative, playful, kind, smart

 Gathering & Organizing

Gather and organize your ideas in the correct spaces.

Topic: All About Me

Topic Sentence
Hello, my name is _____ .
I want to _____ .

How I look
I have _____ eyes and
_____ hair.

What I am like
I am very _____ .
I like to _____ .

Mom says …
I am very _____ .

Concluding Sentence
I think I am _____ .

9

Adding Your Own Ideas

Complete the given topic and concluding sentences or write your own in the blank lines. Then complete the details for the body.

Title

All About Me

Topic Sentence

The first sentence is usually the topic sentence. The topic sentence introduces the topic.

➤ My name is _____. I want to tell you about myself.

Your Own ➤ _____.

Body

The middle sentences are the body. They tell more about the topic.

- I have _____ eyes and _____ hair.
- I am _____ years old, and I am _____ cm tall.
- I am very _____. I like to _____.

Add • I want to be a _____ when I grow up.

Concluding Sentence

The last sentence is the concluding sentence. It ends the paragraph. You can write about your feeling or opinion.

➤ I think I am a great kid because _____.

Your Own ➤ _____.

Word Bank

- **Age:** eight, nine, ten, eleven, twelve
- **Eyes:** big, pretty, small / brown, green, blue
- **Hair:** short, long, curly, straight / blond, black, brown
- **Character:** •creative—come up with different ideas •active—play outside
  •funny—make people laugh •smart—solve problems
  •calm—read books alone •kind—help other people •strong—carry heavy things
- **What Mom says:** always a good boy / girl, sometimes don't listen to her, always a really special boy / girl
- **Reasons:** everybody loves me, I make people happy, I am always happy

My 1st Draft

Rewrite your ideas from the previous page in complete sentences.

All About Me

✔ **Peer Proofreading Checklist:**

- [ ] **Punctuation** ✔capitalization ✔commas(,) ✔periods(.) ✔question marks(?)
- [ ] **Correct spelling**
- [ ] **Complete sentences** S + V + end of sentence

Switch books with your partner and proofread your partner's writing.

↳ After proofreading your 1st draft, rewrite it on your final draft.

Fun Quiz: What is falling from the boy's pocket on page 6?

A: Some _____ are falling. <Answer Key p. 64>

11

Danny's Happy Family

Writing Sprouts

A. Talk about the pictures. Then read the story.

My name is Danny. I want to tell you about my family.

There are four people in my family.

This is my father. He is a brave firefighter.

This is my mother. She is a great pilot.

This is my sister. She is a smart high school student.

And here I am. I am a cheerful elementary school student.

Oh, these are my hamsters, and they are part of my family, too.

My family is so special because they all love me so much.

B. Discuss the questions about the story.

- How many people are there in Danny's family?
- What does Danny's father do?
- What does Danny's mother do?
- What is Danny's sister?
- What is Danny?
- Why is his family so special?

Danny's idea organizer

Topic Sentence
about my family

Parents' Jobs
father — brave firefighter
mother — great pilot

Siblings
sister — smart high
school student

Pets
hamsters

Concluding Sentence
so special because they all love me so much

Key Vocabulary & Expressions

- brave, great, smart, cheerful
- part of one's family

- firefighter, pilot, high school, elementary school
- this is / these are

Hunt for Sentence Parts

Read the story again and do as follows:

1. Draw ⬭circles⬭ on the subjects.
2. Draw ▭rectangles▭ on the verbs.

Example Ⓘ ▭want▭ to tell you about my family.

Subject Ⓢ
Verb Ⓥ

13

C. Ask and answer questions with your partner.

Q: What does she/he do?

She   is   an architect.

Q: What is she/he like?

She   is   very smart.

- Job: (an) architect, office worker, engineer, English teacher
  (a) doctor, chef, pilot, designer, lawyer, firefighter, nurse, math teacher, housewife, police officer
- Character: kind, funny, creative, smart, active, brave, cool, shy, friendly, hardworking

D. Look at the pictures and complete the sentences with the ideas from activity C.

1  **2**  **3**  **4**

1. He is a _____. He is very _____.

2. She is a _____. She is very _____.

3. My uncle is a _____. He is very _____.

4. My mom is a _____. She is very _____.

Writing Process

 **Planning**

Brainstorm and write your ideas. Any idea is all right.

——————————   ——————————

——————————   ——————————

——————————   ——————————

Topic
My Happy Family

Word Bank

- Job: doctor, chef, pilot, designer, lawyer, firefighter, nurse, math teacher, housewife, police officer
- Character: kind, strong, funny, creative, smart, active, calm, cool
- Pet: puppy, kitten, hamster, turtle, lizard, bird
- Specialty: try to spend time together, try to understand each other, try to share everything, love to talk about our problems and solve them together

Gathering & Organizing

Gather and organize your ideas in the correct spaces.

Topic: My Happy Family

Topic Sentence
Hello. My name is _____ .
I'd like to tell you about _____
_____ .

Parents' Jobs
My father is a _____ .
He is very _____ .
My mother is a _____ .
She is very _____ .

Siblings
I have _____ ,
and she/he is _____ .

Pets
I have a pet. It is a _____ . /
I don't have a pet, but I want a _____
_____ .

Concluding Sentence
My family is so special because we _____ .

15

Adding Your Own Ideas

Complete the given topic and concluding sentences or write your own in the blank lines. Then complete the details for the body.

Title

My Happy Family

Topic Sentence

The first sentence is usually the topic sentence. The topic sentence introduces the topic.

↳ My name is _____. I'd like to introduce my family to you.

Your Own ↳ _____ .

Body

The middle sentences are the body. They tell more about the topic.

- There are _____ people in my family.
- My father is a/an _____ . He is very _____ .
- My mother is a/an _____ . She is very _____ .
- My brother is a/an _____ . He is _____ .
- I am a/an _____ . I am very _____ .
- I have a pet. It is a _____ . /
  I don't have a pet, but I want a _____ .

Add
- I love my family, and my family _____ .

Concluding Sentence

The last sentence is the concluding sentence. It ends the paragraph. You can write about your feeling or opinion.

↳ My family is so special because we try to spend time together.

Your Own ↳ _____ .

Word Bank

- **Job:** (an) architect, office worker, engineer, (a) doctor, chef, pilot, designer, lawyer, firefighter, nurse, teacher, housewife, police officer
- **Character:** kind, strong, funny, creative, smart, active, calm, cool
- **Student:** elementary/middle/high school student
- **Pet:** puppy, kitten, hamster, turtle, lizard, bird
- **Speciality:** try to spend time together, try to understand each other, try to share everything, love to talk about our problems and solve them together

My 1st Draft

Rewrite your ideas from the previous page in complete sentences.

My Happy Family

....

....

....

....

....

....

....

....

....

....

....

....

....

....

✔**Peer Proofreading Checklist:**

- [ ] **Punctuation** ✔capitalization ✔commas(,) ✔periods(.) ✔question marks(?)
- [ ] **Correct spelling**
- [ ] **Complete sentences** S + V + end of sentence

Switch books with your partner and proofread your partner's writing.

➥ After proofreading your 1st draft, rewrite it on your final draft.

Fun Quiz: What is Danny holding in his hands on page 12?

A: He is holding _____. <Answer Key p. 64>

UNIT 3 Sarah's Favorite Day

Writing Sprouts

A. Talk about the pictures. Then read the story.

My favorite day is Saturday.

I don't have school on Saturday.

Everyone is home on that day.

My mom cooks waffles for us. They are delicious.

My dad takes us out. We do many interesting things.

In the spring, we fly kites together.

In the summer, we swim in a pool.

In the fall, we take walks in the park.

In the winter, we make a snowman.

Saturday is really special because

my family can do fun things together.

B. Discuss the questions about the story.

- What is Sarah's favorite day of the week?
- What does Sarah's mom cook for the family on Saturday?
- Where does Sarah's dad take the family?
- What do they do in the spring?
- What do they do in the summer?
- What do they do in the fall and winter?
- Why is Saturday special for Sarah?

Sarah's idea organizer

Topic Sentence
My favorite day is Saturday.

Reason 1
I don't have school on Saturday.

Reason 2
My mom cooks waffles.

Reason 3
Dad takes us out. We do many interesting things.

Concluding Sentence
Saturday is really special because my family can do fun things together.

Key Vocabulary & Expressions

- waffle(s)
- cook(s), fly (flies) kites, swim(s), take(s) walks, make(s), can do
- favorite, delicious, special

Hunt for Sentence Parts

Read the story again and do as follows:

1. Draw circles on the subjects.
2. Draw rectangles on the verbs.

Example **My favorite day is Saturday.**

Subject Ⓢ
Verb Ⓥ

C. Ask and answer questions with your partner.

Q: Which one is your favorite day, Saturday or Sunday? Why?

Saturday
Sunday
is
my favorite day
because I can go to the movies.

- sleep over at my friend's house, bake cookies with Mom, visit my grandparents' house
- play computer games, play sports at the park
- go camping in the mountains, go shopping with Mom
- go to an amusement park, go to the beach

D. Look at the pictures and complete the sentences with the ideas from activity C.

1  **2**  **3**  **4**

1. Saturday is my favorite day because I can _____.

2. Sunday is my favorite day because I can _____.

3. Sunday is a special day because I can _____.

4. Saturday is a special day because I can _____.

Writing Process

Planning

Brainstorm and write your ideas. Any idea is all right.

_____

_____

_____

Topic
My Favorite Day
Saturday/Sunday

_____

_____

_____

Word Bank

- Places: park, movie theater, amusement park, library, country
- Activities: ride(s) a bike, swim(s) in a pool, go(es) to the beach, go(es) to the mountains, go(es) skateboarding, rake(s) leaves, collect(s) beautiful leaves
- Reasons: my family can spend time together, we can enjoy delicious meals, we can do a lot of things together

Gathering & Organizing

Gather and organize your ideas in the correct spaces.

Topic: My Favorite Day

Topic Sentence
My favorite day is
_____ .

Reason 1
There is no class on
_____ .

Reason 2
My mom usually
_____ .

Reason 3
My dad usually takes us to
_____ .
We _____ .

Concluding Sentence
_____ is special because _____ .

Adding Your Own Ideas

Complete the given topic and concluding sentences or write your own in the blank lines. Then complete the details for the body.

Title

My Favorite Day

Topic Sentence

The first sentence is usually the topic sentence. The topic sentence introduces the topic.

➻ My favorite day is _____

_____ .

Your Own ➻ _____

_____

Body

The middle sentences are the body. They tell more about the topic.

• My mom _____ .

• In the spring, my family _____ .

• In the summer, my family _____ .

• In the fall, my family _____ .

• In the winter, my family _____ .

Add • There are so many things I can do on _____ .

Concluding Sentence

The last sentence is the concluding sentence. It ends the paragraph. You can write about your feeling or opinion.

➻ _____ is my favorite day because

_____ .

Your Own ➻ _____

_____ .

Word Bank

• **Places:** the park, a movie theater, an amusement park, the library, the countryside
• **Activities:** plant(s) flowers/trees, go(es) on a picnic, play(s) sports, clean(s) the house, ride(s) a bike, swim(s) in a pool, go(es) to the beach, go(es) to the mountains, travel(s) abroad, rake(s) leaves, collect(s) beautiful leaves
• **Reasons:** my family can spend time together, we can enjoy delicious meals, we can do a lot of things together

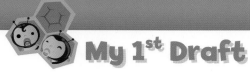

My 1st Draft

Rewrite your ideas from the previous page in complete sentences.

> ## My Favorite Day

✔ Peer Proofreading Checklist:

☐ **Punctuation** ✔capitalization ✔commas(,) ✔periods(.) ✔question marks(?)
☐ **Correct spelling**
☐ **Complete sentences** S + V + end of sentence

Switch books with your partner and proofread your partner's writing.

↪ After proofreading your 1st draft, rewrite it on your final draft.

Fun Quiz: What month is it on Sarah's calendar on page 18?

A: It is _____. <Answer Key p. 64>

23

Sue's Dream House

Writing Sprouts

A. Talk about the pictures. Then read the story.

My dream house is a big wonderful mansion.

It has ten bedrooms and five bathrooms.

A white grand piano is in the living room.

Millions of interesting books are in the study.

A tall refrigerator with a lot of yummy food is in the kitchen.

A large table for twelve people is in the dining room.

A big swimming pool with a water slide is in the backyard.

Many cool sports cars are in the garage.

Don't you want to come and visit my dream house?

B. **Discuss the questions about the story.**

- What is Sue's dream house?
- How many bedrooms and bathrooms does it have?
- What is in the living room?
- What is in the study?
- How many people can sit at the table in the dining room?
- Where is the big swimming pool?
- What is in the garage?

Sue's idea organizer

Topic Sentence
dream house—a mansion with ten bedrooms and five bathrooms

Living Room, Study
a white grand piano, interesting books

Kitchen, Dining Room
a tall refrigerator, a large table

Backyard, Garage
a big swimming pool, cool sports cars

Concluding Sentence
visit my dream house

Key Vocabulary & Expressions

- dream house, mansion, bedroom(s), bathroom(s), living room, study, kitchen, dining room, backyard, garage, grand piano, refrigerator, table, swimming pool, water slide, sports car(s)
- interesting, cool
- visit, millions of

Hunt for Sentence Parts

Read the story again and do as follows:

1. Draw circles on the subjects.
2. Draw rectangles on the verbs.

Example My dream house is a big wonderful mansion.

Subject S
Verb V

C. Ask and answer questions with your partner.

Q: What is in your dream house?

A white grand piano **is** in the living room.

a comfortable bed in the bedroom, a huge tub in the bathroom, a white grand piano in the living room, a lot of books in the study, a large table in the dining room, a tall refrigerator in the kitchen, a swimming pool in the backyard, many cars in the garage

D. Look at the pictures and complete the sentences with the ideas from activity C.

1  **2**  **3**  **4**

1. There is _____.

2. There is _____.

3. There are _____.

4. There are _____.

Writing Process

 **Planning**

Brainstorm and write your ideas. Any idea is all right.

_____   _____

_____   _____

_____   _____

Topic
My Dream House

Word Bank

- **Dream house:** a mansion, a castle, a treehouse, a cottage by the sea, a penthouse apartment, a two-story house, a log house in the woods, an igloo, a straw hut, a beach house
- **Things your dream house has:** a comfortable sofa, an armchair, a big-screen TV, lots of books, a tall refrigerator, a shiny stove, a big oven, a table with six chairs, a big swimming pool, a nice tennis court, cool cars, a sports car, a fancy computer, a rocking chair, a huge bathtub

 **Gathering & Organizing**

Gather and organize your ideas in the correct spaces.

Topic Sentence

My dream house is _____.
It has _____ bedrooms and _____ bathrooms.

Living Room, Study	**Kitchen, Dining Room**	**Backyard, Garage**
There is/are _____ _____ in the living room. There is/are _____ _____ in the study.	There is/are _____ _____ in the kitchen. There is/are _____ _____ in the dining room.	There is/are _____ _____ in the backyard. There is/are _____ _____ in the garage.

Concluding Sentence

Come and visit my _____.

Adding Your Own Ideas

Complete the given topic and concluding sentences or write your own in the blank lines. Then complete the details for the body.

My Dream House

Title

Topic Sentence

The first sentence is usually the topic sentence. The topic sentence introduces the topic.

↘ My dream house is _____.

It has _____ bedrooms and _____ bathrooms.

Your Own ↘ _____.

Body

The middle sentences are the body. They tell more about the topic.

• There is/are _____ in the living room.

• There is/are _____ in the study.

• There is/are _____ in the kitchen.

• There is/are _____ in the dining room.

• There is/are _____ in the backyard.

• There is/are _____ in the garage.

Add • Most important of all, there is my lovely family in my _____

_____.

Concluding Sentence

The last sentence is the concluding sentence. It ends the paragraph. You can write about your feeling or opinion.

↘ Don't you want to visit my _____?

Your Own ↘ _____.

Word Bank

• **Dream house:** a mansion, a castle, a treehouse, a cottage by the sea, a penthouse apartment, a two-story house, a log house in the woods, an igloo, a straw hut, a beach house

• **Things your dream house has:** a comfortable sofa, a white grand piano, an armchair, a big-screen TV, lots of books, a bookshelf with many books, a tall refrigerator, a shiny stove, a microwave oven, a big oven, a large table, a table with six chairs, a big swimming pool, a nice tennis court, a fish pond, many trees, cool cars, a sports car, a bicycle, a fancy computer, a cozy bed, a rocking chair, a huge bathtub, a desk, a nice garden

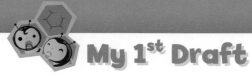 **My 1ˢᵗ Draft**

Rewrite your ideas from the previous page in complete sentences.

My Dream House

✔ Peer Proofreading Checklist:

☐ **Punctuation** ✔capitalization ✔commas(,) ✔periods(.) ✔question marks(?)
☐ **Correct spelling**
☐ **Complete sentences** S + V + end of sentence

Switch books with your partner and proofread your partner's writing.

↪ After proofreading your 1ˢᵗ draft, rewrite it on your final draft.

Fun Quiz: How many cars can you see on page 24?

A: I can see _____. <Answer Key p. 64>

S (Subject)

I
My name
My mom/dad
My family
This/These
That/Those
Everybody

V (Verb)

make(s)
want(s)
think(s)
like(s)
love(s)
have (has)

V

am
is
are

O (Object)

to tell you about my family/myself
brown eyes and blond hair
listening to my friends
that I am a great kid
people laugh
us/me

C (Complement)

John/Sue/Betty/Helen/Randy
nine years old
an architect, a chef, a designer
a student
creative/brave/smart
a great kid/a wonderful child
my dad/mom/sister/brother
my hamsters

sticker

sticker

sticker Activity cards are available at the back of the book.

A. Using the words and phrases on p. 30, complete the sentences below. There may be more than one answer.

1. I am _____.

2. My dad/mom is _____.

3. These are _____.

4. I make _____.

5. I want _____.

6. My dad/mom loves _____.

7. My family makes _____.

8. My dad/mom likes _____.

9. I have _____.

10. She thinks _____.

B. Complete the sentences using the phrases from the box below.

1. _____ about myself.

2. I think I am a great kid because _____

   _____.

3. My family is so special because _____.

4. _____ about my family.

5. My mother says that _____.

- I'm cute and funny, but I often don't listen to her
- Let me tell you
- everybody loves me
- we try to understand each other
- I'm going to tell you

S (Subject)

I
My favorite day
Everyone
My mom/dad
My family
My dream house
It
We
They

V (Verb)

play(s)
cook(s)
take(s)
go (goes)
fly (flies)

can do

V

am
is
are

O (Object)

walks
sports/fun games
delicious waffles
camping
fun things
kites

C (Complement)

special
Saturday/Sunday
a big wonderful mansion
home on Sunday

sticker

sticker

 Activity cards are available at the back of the book.

A. Using the words and phrases on p. 32, complete the sentences below. There may be more than one answer.

1. I am _____.

2. My favorite day is _____.

3. My dream house is _____.

4. We are _____.

5. My family can do _____.

6. Everyone plays _____.

7. My mom/dad cooks _____.

8. They take _____.

9. My family goes _____.

10. Everyone flies _____.

B. Complete the sentences using the phrases from the box below.

1. My dream house has _____.

2. Saturday is really special because _____

    _____.

3. My dream house is _____.

4. Don't you want to _____?

5. My favorite day is Sunday because _____.

- a huge castle
- a big swimming pool in the backyard
- my family can spend time together
- come and visit my cottage by the sea
- I don't have school on Saturday

My Favorite Animal

Writing Sprouts

A. Talk about the pictures. Then read the story.

My favorite animal is a giraffe.

Giraffes are amazing animals.

I like giraffes because they are so tall.

They can eat leaves and fruit from the branches of tall trees.

I like giraffes because they are so strong.

They can kick with their legs and scare away their enemies.

I like giraffes because they are so beautiful.

They have long necks, brown spots, and big eyes.

Giraffes are tall, strong, and beautiful.

That's why I like them the best.

B. Discuss the questions about the story.

- What is the girl's favorite animal?
- How can giraffes eat from tall trees?
- What can giraffes do with their legs?
- What makes giraffes so beautiful?
- Why is the giraffe the girl's favorite animal?

> The girl's idea organizer

Topic Sentence

My favorite animal is a giraffe.

What they can do	**Other things they can do**	**How they look**
tall—eat leaves, branches, and fruit from tall trees	strong—kick with their legs and scare away their enemies	beautiful—have long necks, brown spots, and big eyes

Concluding Sentence

I like them the best.

Key Vocabulary & Expressions

- amazing, tall, strong
- kick, scare away, That's why…
- leaf (leaves), branch (branches), spot (spots), enemy (enemies)

Hunt for Sentence Parts

Read the story again and do as follows:

1. Draw circles on the subjects.
2. Draw rectangles on the verbs.

Example   My favorite animal is a giraffe.

Subject Ⓢ
Verb Ⓥ

C. Ask and answer questions with your partner.

Q: What is your favorite animal and why?

I   like   giraffes   because they are so tall.

Q: What can they do?

They   can eat   leaves   from tall trees.

- • Animals: eagle(s), horse(s), monkey(s), lion(s), whale(s)
- • Characteristics: so powerful, so fast, so clever, so cute, so smart, so strong, so fierce, so big, so lovable
- • What they can do: fly very high in the sky, run very fast, climb trees very well, roar very loudly, hunt with sharp teeth and claws, swim very fast in the ocean, hold their breath underwater for a long time

D. Look at the pictures and complete the sentences with the ideas from activity C.

1. Horses are my favorite animals because they are _____.
   They can _____.

2. Monkeys are my favorite animals because they are _____.
   They can _____.

3. Whales are my favorite animals because they are _____.
   They can _____.

4. Eagles are my favorite animals because they are _____.
   They can _____.

Writing Process

 **Planning**

Brainstorm and write your ideas. Any idea is all right.

_____   _____

_____   _____

_____   _____

Topic
My Favorite Animal

Word Bank

- Animals: eagle(s), horse(s), lion(s), whale(s)
- Characteristics: so beautiful, so powerful, so fast, so clever, so strong, so fierce, so big, so lovable
- What they can do: fly very high in the sky, hunt with their pointed beaks, run very fast, kick their enemies away with their back legs, roar very loudly, hunt with sharp teeth and claws, swim very fast in the ocean, hold their breath underwater for a long time
- How they look: large wings, lovely feathers, long manes, human-like faces, golden manes, long fangs, special blowholes, huge tail fins

 **Gathering & Organizing**

Gather and organize your ideas in the correct spaces.

Topic Sentence

My favorite animal is a(an) _____.

What they can do	Other things they can do	How they look
They are _____.	They are _____.	They are _____.
They can _____	They can _____	They have _____
_____	_____	_____
_____.	_____.	_____.

Concluding Sentence

I like _____ the best.

Adding Your Own Ideas

Complete the given topic and concluding sentences or write your own in the blank lines. Then complete the details for the body.

Title

My Favorite Animal

Topic Sentence

The first sentence is usually the topic sentence. The topic sentence introduces the topic.

↳ I love all animals, but my favorite animal is a(n) _____.

Your Own ↳ _____.

Body

The middle sentences are the body. They tell more about the topic.

- I like _____ because they are _____.
- They can _____.
- I like _____ because they are _____.
- They can _____.
- I like _____ because they are _____.
- They can _____.

Add
- I love _____ because they are the most interesting animals.

Concluding Sentence

The last sentence is the concluding sentence. It ends the paragraph. You can write about your feeling or opinion.

↳ My favorite animal is _____.

because they are _____, _____, and _____.

Your Own ↳ _____.

Word Bank

- **Animals:** eagle(s), horse(s), lion(s), whale(s)
- **Characteristics:** so beautiful, so powerful, so fast, so clever, so strong, so fierce, so big, so lovable
- **What they can do:** fly very high in the sky, hunt with their pointed beaks, run very fast, kick their enemies away with their back legs, roar very loudly, hunt with sharp teeth and claws, swim very fast in the ocean, hold their breath underwater for a long time
- **How they look:** large wings, lovely feathers, long manes, human-like faces, golden manes, long fangs, special blowholes, huge tail fins

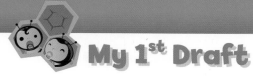 **My 1ˢᵗ Draft**

Rewrite your ideas from the previous page in complete sentences.

> ## My Favorite Animal

✔ **Peer Proofreading Checklist:**

- [ ] **Punctuation** ✔capitalization ✔commas(,) ✔periods(.) ✔question marks(?)
- [ ] **Correct spelling**
- [ ] **Complete sentences** S + V + end of sentence

Switch books with your partner and proofread your partner's writing.

↪ After proofreading your 1ˢᵗ draft, rewrite it on your final draft.

Fun Quiz: What is the giraffe kicking on page 34?

A: It is _____ away. <Answer Key p. 64>

Mom's Magic Kitchen

Writing Sprouts

A. Talk about the pictures. Then read the story.

My mom's kitchen is an amazing place.

It is like a magic box.

She has a fancy stove and a huge oven.

She has shiny pans and large pots.

Every morning, I can smell sweet pancakes.

Every evening, I can smell delicious foods.

My mom is like a magician.

She turns carrots into sweet carrot cake.

She turns broccoli into delicious broccoli soup.

She turns apples into yummy apple pie.

I love to help my mom in her special kitchen.

B. Discuss the questions about the story.

- Why does the girl think her mom's kitchen is an amazing place?
- What does her mom have in her kitchen?
- What can the girl smell every morning?
- What can the girl smell every evening?
- Why does the girl think her mom is like a magician?
- What does the girl love to do in the kitchen?

> The girl's idea organizer

Topic Sentence

Mom's kitchen is an amazing place, a magic box

I see	**I smell**	**I feel**
a stove, an oven, pans, and pots	sweet pancakes, delicious foods	Mom is like a magician

Concluding Sentence

love to help my mom

Key Vocabulary & Expressions

- amazing, fancy, huge, shiny, large
- turn(s)...into
- like a magic box, like a magician

Hunt for Sentence Parts

Read the story again and do as follows:

1. Draw circles on the subjects.
2. Draw rectangles on the verbs.

Example My mom's kitchen is an amazing place.

Subject Ⓢ
Verb Ⓥ

41

C. Ask and answer questions with your partner.

Q: What is she/he like?

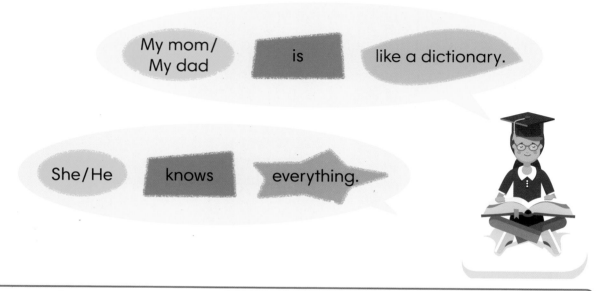

My mom/ My dad **is** like a dictionary.

She/He **knows** everything.

- like Superman—always save(s) me
- like a model—walk(s) in a strange way
- like a movie star—is good-looking
- like a calculator—can solve math problems quickly

- like a horse—run(s) very fast
- like a mule—is very stubborn

D. Look at the pictures and complete the sentences with the ideas from activity C.

①  **②**  **③**  **④**

1. My brother is _____. He _____.

2. My dad is _____. He _____.

3. My sister is _____. She _____.

4. My uncle is _____. He _____.

Writing Process

Brainstorm and write your ideas. Any idea is all right.

Topic
Mom's Magic Kitchen

Word Bank

- Mom's kitchen: neat and special, bright and warm, nice and pleasant
- Kitchen items: a fancy stove and a huge oven, pretty dishes and fancy bowls
- Food: sweet pancakes, delicious omelets, spaghetti with meat sauce, delicious stew
- Mom's special food: bread, meat pies, apple pies, cookies, steak, stew, spaghetti, hot dogs
- What I like to do: help my mom cook, watch my mom cook, wash the dishes, set the table

 Gathering & Organizing

Gather and organize your ideas in the correct spaces.

Topic: **Mom's Magic Kitchen**

Topic Sentence
My mom's kitchen is very _____.

I see	I smell	I feel
She has _____ _____ _____. She also has _____ _____ _____.	Every morning, I can smell _____ _____. Every evening, I can smell _____ _____.	My mom is the best cook. She always cooks delicious foods. Her special food is _____. It is the most delicious food in the world.

Concluding Sentence
I love to _____ in the kitchen.

Adding Your Own Ideas

Complete the given topic and concluding sentences or write your own in the blank lines. Then complete the details for the body.

Title

Mom's Magic Kitchen

Topic Sentence

The first sentence is usually the topic sentence. The topic sentence introduces the topic.

➤ My mom's kitchen is always very _____.

Your Own ➤ _____

_____

Body

The middle sentences are the body. They tell more about the topic.

- In the kitchen, I can see _____.
- She also has _____.
- Every morning, I can smell _____.
- Every evening, I can smell _____.
- My mom is the best cook in the world. She always cooks delicious foods. Her special food is _____.
  It is the most delicious food.

Add - When I grow up, I want to _____.

Concluding Sentence

The last sentence is the concluding sentence. It ends the paragraph. You can write about your feeling or opinion.

➤ I really love to _____

_____

Your Own ➤ _____

Word Bank

- **Mom's kitchen:** neat and special, bright and warm, nice and pleasant
- **Kitchen items:** a fancy stove and a huge oven, shiny pans and large pots, a nice microwave and a cool blender, pretty dishes and shiny bowls
- **Food:** sweet pancakes, delicious omelets, fried and boiled eggs, yummy waffles, meat pies, fresh juice, spaghetti with meat sauce, delicious stew, rice and soup, yummy steak
- **Mom's special food:** bread, meat pies, apple pies, cookies, steak, stew, spaghetti, hot dogs
- **What I like to do:** help my mom cook, watch my mom cook, wash the dishes, set the table

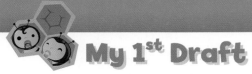 **My 1st Draft**

Rewrite your ideas from the previous page in complete sentences.

Mom's Magic Kitchen

✔ **Peer Proofreading Checklist:**

- [ ] **Punctuation** ✔capitalization ✔commas(,) ✔periods(.) ✔question marks(?)
- [ ] **Correct spelling**
- [ ] **Complete sentences** S + V + end of sentence

Switch books with your partner and proofread your partner's writing.

↳ After proofreading your 1st draft, rewrite it on your final draft.

Fun Quiz: What is on Mom's dress on page 40?

A: There are _____ on her dress. <Answer Key p. 64>

How to Cook Hot Dogs

Writing Sprouts

A. Talk about the pictures. Then read the story.

I like to eat hot dogs because they are delicious and easy to cook. You need sausages, hot dog buns, onions, ketchup, and pickles.

There are five steps to make a good hot dog.

First, heat a pot of water and put the sausages in the pot.

Second, boil the sausages for about five to six minutes.

Be careful or you might get burned.

Third, take out the sausages from the pot.

After that, put one of the sausages on a bun.

Finally, add some ketchup, onions, and pickles.

Now you are ready to enjoy the tasty hot dog.

B. Discuss the questions about the story.

- Why does the boy like to eat hot dogs?
- What do you need to make hot dogs?
- What is the first step?
- What are the second and third steps?
- What is the next step?
- What is the last step?

The boy's idea organizer

Topic Sentence

hot dogs are delicious and easy to cook

First, heat a pot of water.

Second, boil the sausages.

Third, take out the sausages.

Finally, add some ketchup, onions, and pickles.

After that, put one of the sausages on a bun.

Concluding Sentence

ready to enjoy the tasty hot dog

Key Vocabulary & Expressions

- sausages, hot dog buns
- first, second, third, after that, finally
- heat, boil, be careful, take out, put, add, be ready to enjoy
- Be careful or you might get burned.

Hunt for Sentence Parts

Read the story again and do as follows:

1. Draw circles on the subjects.
2. Draw rectangles on the verbs.

Example I like to eat hot dogs.

Subject Ⓢ
Verb Ⓥ

47

C. Ask and answer questions with your partner.

Q: How do I cook delicious cheeseburgers by myself?

You → need → some burger patties, hamburger buns, sliced tomatoes, sliced onions, lettuce, and cheese.

- add some ketchup, pickles, and mayonnaise
- place a slice of tomato, a slice of onion, and some lettuce on the cheese
- heat the burger patties in a hot pan and cook them for 3 to 5 minutes
- put a cooked patty and a slice of cheese on a hamburger bun

D. Look at the pictures and complete the sentences with the ideas from activity C.

❶  ❷  ❸  ❹

1. First, heat _____

   _____.

2. Second, put _____

   _____.

3. Third, place _____

   _____.

4. Finally, add _____

   _____.

Writing Process

Planning

Brainstorm and write your ideas. Any idea is all right.

_____

_____

_____

Topic
How to Cook Delicious Food
(Cheeseburger)

_____

_____

_____

Word Bank

- **Order:** first, second, third, after that, finally
- **Action:** heat, cook, take out, put, place, add, be ready to enjoy
- **Ingredients:** hamburger buns, burger patties, one or two slices of cheese, sliced tomatoes, sliced onions, lettuce, ketchup, pickles, mayonnaise

Gathering & Organizing

Gather and organize your ideas in the correct spaces.

Topic: How to Cook Cheeseburgers

Topic Sentence

I love to eat cheeseburgers, and they are easy to cook.

You need _____	First, heat _____	Second, put _____
_____	_____	_____
_____ .	_____ .	_____ .

Finally, add _____	Third, place _____
_____	_____
_____ .	_____ .

Concluding Sentence

Now you are ready to enjoy the _____ .

Adding Your Own Ideas

Complete the given topic and concluding sentences or write your own in the blank lines. Then complete the details for the body.

Title

How to Cook Cheeseburgers

Topic Sentence

The first sentence is usually the topic sentence. The topic sentence introduces the topic.

↳ Cheeseburgers are _____
_____.

Your Own ↳ _____.

Body

The middle sentences are the body. They tell more about the topic.

• You need hamburger buns, meat patties, one or two slices of cheese, sliced tomatoes, sliced onions, lettuce, ketchup, pickles, and mayonnaise.

• First, heat _____.

• Second, put _____.

• Third, place _____.

• Finally, add _____.

Add • Now add a handful of crunchy potato chips to go with your _____
_____.

Concluding Sentence

The last sentence is the concluding sentence. It ends the paragraph. You can write about your feeling or opinion.

↳ The cheeseburger is now ready to _____
_____.

Your Own ↳ _____.

Word Bank

• Procedures:
  First, heat the burger patties in the hot pan and cook them for 3 to 5 minutes.
  Second, put a cooked patty and a slice of cheese on a hamburger bun.
  Third, place a slice of tomato, a slice of onion, and some lettuce on the cheese.
  Finally, add some ketchup, pickles, and mayonnaise.

My 1st Draft

Rewrite your ideas from the previous page in complete sentences.

How to Cook Cheeseburgers

✔ **Peer Proofreading Checklist:**

- ☐ **Punctuation** ✔capitalization ✔commas(,) ✔periods(.) ✔question marks(?)
- ☐ **Correct spelling**
- ☐ **Complete sentences** S + V + end of sentence

Switch books with your partner and proofread your partner's writing.

↪ After proofreading your 1st draft, rewrite it on your final draft.

Fun Quiz: What color is the boy's hair on page 46?

A: It is _____. <Answer Key p. 64>

51

What Drones Can Do

Writing Sprouts

A. Talk about the pictures. Then read the story.

What are drones, and what can they do?

Drones are like flying robots.

Drones are useful and amazing. They can do many things.

First, drones can take pictures and videos in the air.

People don't have to fly to the sky to take pictures.

Next, drones can make people safer in many ways.

Drones can search for people who are lost.

Drones can watch for wildfires or floods.

Lastly, drones can even deliver things to our homes.

Drones can deliver food or packages to people.

I believe that someday drones will be as important as cars.

B. Discuss the questions about the story.

- What are drones?
- What are three things that drones can do for us now?
- What are some things drones might be able to do in the future?

The boy's idea organizer

Topic Sentence
Drones are useful
and amazing

First,
can take pictures
and videos

Next,
can make people
safer in many ways

Lastly,
can deliver food or
packages

Concluding Sentence
drones will be as important as cars

Key Vocabulary & Expressions

- drone(s), flying robot(s), wildfire(s), package(s), flood(s)
- take pictures/videos, search for, watch for, deliver

- useful, safe/safer
- someday, ...as important as...

Hunt for Sentence Parts

Read the story again and do as follows:

1. Draw circles on the subjects.
2. Draw rectangles on the verbs.

Example What are drones, and what can they do?

Subject Ⓢ
Verb Ⓥ

C. Ask and answer questions with your partner.

Q: What is going to change the way we take photos?

Drones   are going to change   the way we take photos.

- Robots—the way we take care of sick people, the way we protect ourselves
- 3D printers—the way we design things, the way we make stuff
- Self-driving cars—the way we drive, the way we get around

D. Look at the pictures and complete the sentences with the ideas from activity C.

1. 3D printers will change _____.

2. Robots will change _____.

3. Self-driving cars will change _____.

4. Robots will change _____.

Writing Process

 **Planning**

Brainstorm and write your ideas. Any idea is all right.

_____   _____

_____   _____

_____   _____

Topic
What Robots Can Do

Word Bank

- Robots can help people clean: can dust and mop the floors, can wash the windows of tall buildings
- Robots can save people who are in danger: can search for survivors in an earthquake, can look for hikers who are lost in the mountains
- Robots can work on a farm and help the farmers: can drive tractors and do farm work, take care of crops
- I think that: robots will be as useful as computers, robots will be as important as cars

 Gathering & Organizing

Gather and organize your ideas in the correct spaces.

Topic: What Robots Can Do

Topic Sentence
What are robots, and what can they do? Robots are like humans. Robots are useful and amazing.

First,
robots can help people clean.
_____
_____

Next,
robots can save people who are in danger. _____
_____
_____

Lastly,
robots can work on a farm and help the farmers. _____
_____
_____

Concluding Sentence
I think that robots _____ .

Adding Your Own Ideas

Complete the given topic and concluding sentences or write your own in the blank lines. Then complete the details for the body.

Title

What Robots Can Do

Topic Sentence

The first sentence is usually the topic sentence. The topic sentence introduces the topic.

➔ Robots are really cool. They can _____
_____ .

Your Own ➔ _____ .

Body

The middle sentences are the body. They tell more about the topic.

• First, robots can help people clean.
_____ .

• Next, robots can save people who are in danger.
_____ .

• Lastly, robots can work on a farm and help the farmers.
_____ .

Add • Robots can do all these things, and they will _____
_____ .

Concluding Sentence

The last sentence is the concluding sentence. It ends the paragraph. You can write about your feeling or opinion.

➔ I believe that _____
_____ .

Your Own ➔ _____ .

Word Bank

• **Robots can help people clean:** can dust and mop the floors, can wash the windows of tall buildings
• **Robots can save people who are in danger:** can search for survivors in an earthquake, can look for hikers who are lost in the mountains
• **Robots can work on a farm and help the farmers:** can drive tractors and do farm work, can take care of crops
• **I believe that:** robots will be as useful as computers, robots will be as important as cars

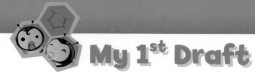

My 1st Draft

Rewrite your ideas from the previous page in complete sentences.

What Robots Can Do

What are robots, and what can they do? Robots are like humans.

✔ **Peer Proofreading Checklist:**

- **Punctuation** ✔capitalization ✔commas(,) ✔periods(.) ✔question marks(?)
- **Correct spelling**
- **Complete sentences** S + V + end of sentence

Switch books with your partner and proofread your partner's writing.

↳ After proofreading your 1st draft, rewrite it on your final draft.

Fun Quiz: What is the yellow drone carrying on page 52?

A: It is carrying _____. <Answer Key p. 64>

S (Subject)

I
She/He
They
We
It
My mother's kitchen
My favorite animal
Giraffes/Whales

V (Verb)

like(s)
have (has)
love(s)

can eat
can kick
can smell

V

am
is
are

O (Object)

to help my mother
a fancy stove and a huge oven
eagles/monkeys/lions/
horses/whales
leaves, branches, and fruit
their enemies
sweet pancakes

C (Complement)

a horse/a whale
like a magic box
amazing animals
like a magician
an amazing place

sticker

sticker

Activity cards are available at the back of the book.

A. Using the words and phrases on p. 58, complete the sentences below. There may be more than one answer.

1. She is _____.

2. Whales are _____.

3. Giraffes can eat _____.

4. Giraffes can kick _____.

5. I can smell _____.

6. I like _____.

7. She likes _____.

8. They have _____.

9. He loves _____.

10. They love _____.

B. Complete the sentences using the phrases from the box below.

1. _____ a giraffe.

2. My favorite animal is a whale because _____

    _____.

3. My mother's kitchen is always _____.

4. _____ in the kitchen.

5. _____ I like them the best.

- they are so big, but they can swim very fast in the ocean
- warm and welcoming
- I love all animals, but my favorite animal is
- I really love to help my mother cook
- That's why

O (Object)

to eat hot dogs
sausages and hot dog buns
people safer
people who are lost
wildfires or floods
food or packages
a pot of water
the sausages for five minutes
eating cheeseburgers

S (Subject)

I
You
She/He
They
Drones
Robots

V (Verb)

like(s)
need(s)
heat(s)
boil(s)
enjoy(s)

can make
can watch for
can search for
can deliver

V

am
is
are

C (Complement)

ready to enjoy the tasty hot dog
like flying robots
useful and amazing
as important as cars

sticker

sticker

Activity cards are available at the back of the book.

A. Using the words and phrases on p. 60, complete the sentences below. There may be more than one answer.

1. I am _____.

2. Drones are _____.

3. They can search for _____.

4. Drones can watch for _____.

5. They can deliver _____.

6. She likes _____.

7. You need _____.

8. She heats _____.

9. They boil _____.

10. He enjoys _____.

B. Complete the sentences using the phrases from the box below.

1. _____ because they are delicious and easy to cook.

2. Cheeseburgers are always delicious, and _____

   _____.

3. I believe that _____.

4. Robots _____.

5. _____ to take pictures.

- someday drones will be as important as cars
- I can cook them by myself
- can do a lot of things for people
- I like to eat hot dogs
- People don't have to fly to the sky

Proofreading Help

🍃 Subject-Verb Agreement 1 — "Be" Verbs

I	am am not	
He / She	is is not (isn't)	active.
We / You / They	are are not (aren't)	

There	is is not (isn't)	a large sofa	in the room.
	are are not (aren't)	millions of books	

🍃 Subject-Verb Agreement 2 — Other Verbs

I / You / We / They	have / like / want	a pet. waffles.
He / She	has / likes / wants	

🍃 Subject-Verb Agreement 3 — Helping Verbs

I He / She You / We / They	can cannot (can't)	run	fast.
	will will not (won't)		

Word Form — Plural Nouns

- My favorite animal is <u>a giraffe</u>.
- <u>Giraffe</u>s are amazing <u>animal</u>s.

-s	• nurse → nurse**s** • onion → onion**s**	**-ies**	• patty → patt**ies** • enemy → enem**ies**
-es	• branch → branch**es** • tomato → tomato**es**	**-ves**	• leaf → lea**ves** • wife → wi**ves**
* • person → people		• video → videos	• photo → photos

* Nouns that do NOT have plural forms

soup	a bowl of soup, two bowls of soup, some soup
water	a pot of water, two glasses of water, some water
cheese	a slice of cheese, two slices of cheese, some cheese
some ketchup, some mayonnaise, some lettuce	

 Punctuation

Capitalization	<u>B</u>e careful. (beginning letter of the first word of a sentence) My name is <u>L</u>ucy. (names of people and places) Here <u>I</u> am. (I)
Period	My mom is like a magician<u>.</u> (at the end of a sentence)
Question Mark	What are drones<u>?</u> (at the end of a question)
Comma	First<u>,</u> heat a pot of water. (after *first, second, third, last*) In the spring<u>,</u> we fly kites together. (after time expressions) They have long necks<u>,</u> brown spots<u>,</u> and big eyes. (when three or more words are connected) These are my hamsters<u>,</u> and they are part of my family, too. (when two sentences are connected)
apostrophe	I don<u>'</u>t have school on Sunday. (short form of *do not* or *cannot*) Mom<u>'</u>s kitchen is an amazing place. (to show what belongs to someone)

Answer Key

Unit 1 All About Me ▶p.11

Fun Quiz: What is falling from the boy's pocket on page 6?
A: Some candies are falling.

Unit 2 Danny's Happy Family ▶p.17

Fun Quiz: What is Danny holding in his hands on page 12?
A: He is holding hamsters.

Unit 3 Sarah's Favorite Day ▶p.23

Fun Quiz: What month is it on Sarah's calendar on page 18?
A: It is March.

Unit 4 Sue's Dream House ▶p.29

Fun Quiz: How many cars can you see on page 24?
A: I can see four cars.

Unit 5 My Favorite Animal ▶p.39

Fun Quiz: What is the giraffe kicking on page 34?
A: It is kicking a lion away.

Unit 6 Mom's Magic Kitchen ▶p.45

Fun Quiz: What is on Mom's dress on page 40?
A: There are strawberries on her dress.

Unit 7 How to Cook Hot Dogs ▶p.51

Fun Quiz: What color is the boy's hair on page 46?
A: It is blond.

Unit 8 What Drones Can Do ▶p.57

Fun Quiz: What is the yellow drone carrying on page 52?
A: It is carrying a package(box).

My name (s) Unit 1	is (v) Unit 1	John/Sue/Betty/Brian/Helen. (c) Unit 1
I (s) Unit 1	am (v) Unit 1	nine years old. (c) Unit 1
I (s) Unit 1	have (v) Unit 1	blue eyes and brown hair. (o) Unit 1
I (s) Unit 1	am (v) Unit 1	creative. (c) Unit 1
She (s) Unit 1	is (v) Unit 1	friendly. (c) Unit 1
I (s) Unit 1	like (v) Unit 1	to make people laugh. (o) Unit 1
My mom (s) Unit 1	says (v) Unit 1	I am smart and funny. (o) Unit 1

Writing Garden Book 1

Writing Garden Book 1

Writing Garden Book 1

Writing Garden Book 1

Writing Garden Book 1

Writing Garden Book 1

Writing Garden Book 1

Writing Garden Book 1

Writing Garden Book 1

Writing Garden Book 1

Writing Garden Book 1

Writing Garden Book 1

Writing Garden Book 1

Writing Garden Book 1

Writing Garden Book 1

Writing Garden Book 1

Writing Garden Book 1

Writing Garden Book 1

s	v	c / o
I	want	to tell you about my family.
My dad	is	a brave firefighter.
My mom	is	a great pilot.
I	am	an elementary school student.
She	is	a high school student.
He	is	a creative architect.
My family	try (tries)	to spend time together.

Unit 2

Writing Garden Book 1

Writing Garden Book 1

Writing Garden Book 1

Writing Garden Book 1

Writing Garden Book 1

Writing Garden Book 1

Writing Garden Book 1

Writing Garden Book 1

Writing Garden Book 1

Writing Garden Book 1

Writing Garden Book 1

Writing Garden Book 1

Writing Garden Book 1

Writing Garden Book 1

Writing Garden Book 1

Writing Garden Book 1

Writing Garden Book 1

Writing Garden Book 1

s	v	o
I	don't have	school on Saturday.
My mom	cook(s)	waffles for us.
My dad	take(s)	us to the park.
We	do	many interesting things.
My family	can do	fun things together.
We	make(s)	a snowman at the park.
We	fly (flies)	kites with other people.

Unit 3

Writing Garden Book 1

Writing Garden Book 1

Writing Garden Book 1

Writing Garden Book 1

Writing Garden Book 1

Writing Garden Book 1

Writing Garden Book 1

Writing Garden Book 1

Writing Garden Book 1

Writing Garden Book 1

Writing Garden Book 1

Writing Garden Book 1

Writing Garden Book 1

Writing Garden Book 1

Writing Garden Book 1

Writing Garden Book 1

Writing Garden Book 1

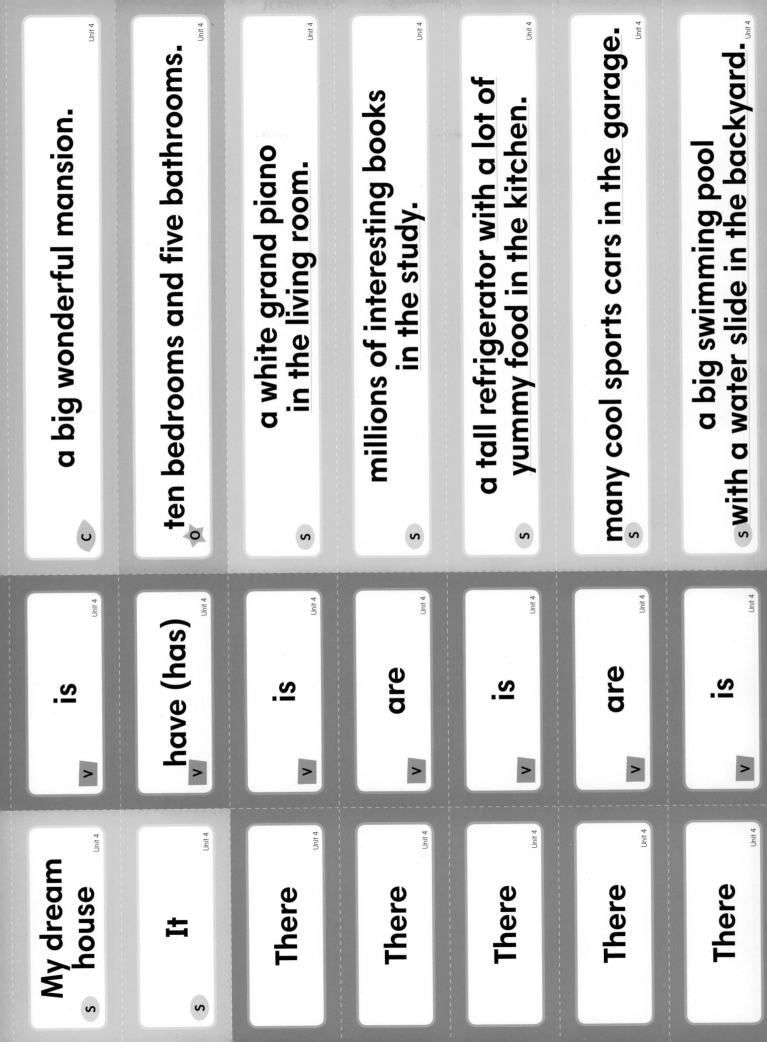

My dream house (s)	is (v)	a big wonderful mansion. (c)
It (s)	have (has) (v)	ten bedrooms and five bathrooms. (o)
There (s)	is (v)	a white grand piano in the living room. (s)
There (s)	are (v)	millions of interesting books in the study. (s)
There (s)	is (v)	a tall refrigerator with a lot of yummy food in the kitchen. (s)
There (s)	are (v)	many cool sports cars in the garage. (s)
There (s)	is (v)	a big swimming pool with a water slide in the backyard. (s)

Unit 4

Writing Garden Book 1

Writing Garden Book 1

Writing Garden Book 1

Writing Garden Book 1

Writing Garden Book 1

Writing Garden Book 1

Writing Garden Book 1

Writing Garden Book 1

Writing Garden Book 1

Writing Garden Book 1

Writing Garden Book 1

Writing Garden Book 1

Writing Garden Book 1

Writing Garden Book 1

Writing Garden Book 1

Writing Garden Book 1

Writing Garden Book 1

Writing Garden Book 1

s	v	c / o
My favorite animal	is	a giraffe.
They	are	amazing animals.
I	like	giraffes because they are so tall.
They	can eat	leaves and fruit from the branches of tall trees.
She	like(s)	horses because they are so fast.
He	like(s)	eagles because they are so powerful.
They	have (has)	long necks, brown spots, and big eyes.

Unit 5

Writing Garden Book 1

Writing Garden Book 1

Writing Garden Book 1

Writing Garden Book 1

Writing Garden Book 1

Writing Garden Book 1

Writing Garden Book 1

Writing Garden Book 1

Writing Garden Book 1

Writing Garden Book 1

Writing Garden Book 1

Writing Garden Book 1

Writing Garden Book 1

Writing Garden Book 1

Writing Garden Book 1

Writing Garden Book 1

Writing Garden Book 1

Writing Garden Book 1

My mom's kitchen (s) — Unit 6	**is** (v) — Unit 6	**an amazing place.** (c) — Unit 6
She (s) — Unit 6	**have (has)** (v) — Unit 6	**a fancy stove and a huge oven.** (o) — Unit 6
She (s) — Unit 6	**have (has)** (v) — Unit 6	**shiny pans and large pots.** (o) — Unit 6
I (s) — Unit 6	**can smell** (v) — Unit 6	**sweet pancakes.** (o) — Unit 6
I (s) — Unit 6	**can smell** (v) — Unit 6	**delicious foods.** (o) — Unit 6
She (s) — Unit 6	**turn(s)** (v) — Unit 6	**carrots into sweet carrot cake.** (o) — Unit 6
I (s) — Unit 6	**love(s)** (v) — Unit 6	**to help mom in her special kitchen.** (o) — Unit 6

Writing Garden Book 1

Writing Garden Book 1

Writing Garden Book 1

Writing Garden Book 1

Writing Garden Book 1

Writing Garden Book 1

Writing Garden Book 1

Writing Garden Book 1

Writing Garden Book 1

Writing Garden Book 1

Writing Garden Book 1

Writing Garden Book 1

Writing Garden Book 1

Writing Garden Book 1

Writing Garden Book 1

Writing Garden Book 1

Writing Garden Book 1

Writing Garden Book 1

Unit 7 flashcards:

- I
- You (Unit 1)
- There
- First,
- Second,
- Third,
- After that,

- like
- need
- are
- heat
- boil
- take out
- put

- to eat hot dogs because they are so delicious.
- sausages, hot dog buns, onions, ketchup, and pickles.
- five steps to make a good hot dog.
- a pot of water.
- the sausages for about five to six minutes.
- the sausages from the pot.
- one of the sausages on a bun.

Writing Garden Book 1

Writing Garden Book 1

Writing Garden Book 1

Writing Garden Book 1

Writing Garden Book 1

Writing Garden Book 1

Writing Garden Book 1

Writing Garden Book 1

Writing Garden Book 1

Writing Garden Book 1

Writing Garden Book 1

Writing Garden Book 1

Writing Garden Book 1

Writing Garden Book 1

Writing Garden Book 1

Writing Garden Book 1

Writing Garden Book 1

Writing Garden Book 1

s	v	c / o
Drones	**are**	**like flying robots.** (c)
They	**are**	**useful and amazing.** (c)
They	**can take**	**pictures and videos in the air.** (o)
People	**don't have to fly**	**to the sky to take pictures.**
They	**can make**	**people safer in many ways.** (o)
They	**can search for**	**people who are lost.** (o)
They	**can deliver**	**food or packages to people.** (o)

Writing Garden Book 1

Writing Garden Book 1

Writing Garden Book 1

Writing Garden Book 1

Writing Garden Book 1

Writing Garden Book 1

Writing Garden Book 1

Writing Garden Book 1

Writing Garden Book 1

Writing Garden Book 1

Writing Garden Book 1

Writing Garden Book 1

Writing Garden Book 1

Writing Garden Book 1

Writing Garden Book 1

Review Stickers

Writing Garden
Workbook
1

J. Randolph Lewis
Lucy Han
Helen Kim

Paragraph Writing

What are drones, and what can they
...are like flying robots.

Writing Garden 1
Written by J. Randolph Lewis, Lucy Han, Helen Kim

Publisher: Anna Park

Project Director: Lucy Han

Content Editor: Kelli Ripatti, Sherry Lee

Designer: Eun Jee Kang

Illustrators: Beehive Illustration (Beatrice Bencivenni, John Lund, Philip Hailstone),
              Jieun Park

Cover Design: Hongdangmoo

ISBN: 979-11-957052-9-0
Photo Credits:
Photos and images © Shutterstock, Inc.

www.runningturtle.co.kr
1203, 36, Hwangsaeul-ro 200beon-gil, Bundang-gu, Seongnam-si,
Gyeonggi-do, KOREA 13595
TEL: +82-2-3452-7979 FAX: +82-31-718-3452

KC This book has been printed with non-toxic materials.

Writing Garden

Workbook 1

 **Sentence Practice**

Put the words in order.

| Subject | + | Verb | + | End of sentence |

1. Brian / is / My name / . /

(My name)   [is]   Brian.

2. funny / very / am / I / . /

(I)   [am]   _____

3. brown hair / have / and / blue eyes / I / . /

(I)   [have]   _____

4. to tell / about / I / want / you / myself / . /

(I)   [want]   _____

5. like to / I / laugh / make people / . /

6. says / I don't listen to her / My mother / . /

7. My mother / I am cute and funny /says / . /

8. old / I / nine years / am / . /

9. love / I / listening / my friends' / to / stories / . /

 **Revising Practice**

Read the story and complete the tasks below.

Title: All About Me

I want to tell you about myself.

Ⓐ My name is ~~david~~.

1. I am nine years old.

2. I have brown eyes and brown hair.

Ⓑ I am very active ○

3. I always like to play outside.

My mother says I am very energetic and independent.

I also love to play sports with my friends.

Ⓒ My mother says I often ~~dont~~ study hard.

A. Correct sentences A, B, and C.

Ⓐ My name is David.

Ⓑ _____

Ⓒ _____

B. Expand sentences 1, 2, and 3 with the given words.

1. (and I am 140 centimeters tall)

I am nine years old, and I am 140 centimeters tall   .

2. (big, long straight)

I have   brown eyes and   brown hair.

3. (with my brother)

I always like to play outside   .

My Final Draft

Title:

<More Than 80 Words>

🌱 **Sentence Practice**

Put the words in order.

Subject ＋ **Verb** ＋ **End of sentence**

1. about / I / to tell / my family / want / you / . /

   (I) [want] to tell you about my family.

2. firefighter / is / He / a / . /

   (He) [is] _____

3. a / student / She / high school / is / . /

   (She) [is] _____

4. so special / is / My family / because / love me / they all / so much / . /

   (My family) [is] _____

5. part of / They / my family, too / are / . /

6. Danny / is / My name / . /

7. my / are / These / hamsters / . /

8. am / an elementary / I / school student / . /

9. is / my / This / mother / . /

Revising Practice

Read the story and complete the tasks below.

Title: Jessica's Happy Family

My name is Jessica. Let me tell you about my family.

A (there) are five people in my family.

1. My father is an architect.

2. My mother is a housewife.

B I have an older sister○

She is a middle school student.

This is my younger sister. She is a preschool student.

And here I am. I am an elementary school student.

C Oh this is my dog, and she is part of my family, too.

3. I love my family, and my family is very special.

A. Correct sentences A, B, and C.

A There are five people in my family.

B _____

C _____

B. Expand sentences 1, 2, and 3 with the given words.

1. (creative)

My father is a very _____ architect.

2. (hardworking)

My mother is a _____ housewife.

3. (we love each other so much)

I love my family, and my family is very special because _____

_____.

My Final Draft

Title:

<More Than 80 Words>

My Comment ☐ Good
☐ Excellent

Parent's Comment ☐ Good ☐ Excellent
Teacher's Comment ☐ Good ☐ Excellent

Sentence Practice

Put the words in order.

| Subject | + | Verb | + | End of sentence |

1. can do / together / is / because / special / my family / fun things / Saturday / . /

   (Saturday) [is] special because my family can do fun things together.

2. home / Everyone / that / is / day / on / . /

   (Everyone) [is] _____

3. us / My dad / takes / out / . /

   (My dad) [takes] _____

4. I / Saturday / on / don't / school / have / . /

   (I) [don't have] _____

5. fly / together / We / kites / . /

6. play / there / We / fun games / . /

7. cooks / us / My mom / waffles / for / . /

8. in / We / a / swim / pool / . /

9. is / favorite day / Saturday / My / . /

Revising Practice

Read the story and complete the tasks below.

Title: Sally's Favorite Day

My favorite day is Saturday.

A I dont have school on Saturday.

I often bake cookies with Mom.

My dad loves to take us outdoors.

B we play fun games there.

1. In the spring, we ride bikes.

2. In the summer, we play badminton.

3. In the fall, we collect beautiful leaves.

C In the winter, we make a snowman

Saturday is a fun day because I can play with my parents.

A. Correct sentences A, B, and C.

A I don't have school on Saturday.

B _____

C _____

B. Expand sentences 1, 2, and 3 with the given words.

1. (with our dad at the park)

In the spring, we ride bikes _____.

2. (with our friends on the playground)

In the summer, we play badminton

_____.

3. (with our cousins in our yard)

In the fall, we collect beautiful leaves

_____.

My Final Draft

Title:

<More Than 90 Words>

Language Sprouts

Sentence Practice

Put the words in order.

| Subject | + | Verb | + | End of sentence |

1. big / is / mansion / My dream house / a / . /

   (My dream house) [is] __a big mansion.__

2. interesting / are / the study / Millions of/ books / in / . /

   (Millions of interesting books) [are] _____

3. is / the living room / grand piano / A / in / white / . /

   (A white grand piano) [is] _____

4. is / a water slide / the backyard / with / in / A big swimming pool / . /

   (A big swimming pool with a water slide) [is] _____

5. ten bedrooms / and / It / has / five bathrooms / . /

   ⬭   ▭   _____

6. the dining room / is / in / A large table for twelve people / . /

   ⬭   ▭   _____

7. Many / the garage / cool / in / are / sports cars / . /

   ⬭   ▭   _____

8. the kitchen / in / is / A tall refrigerator / yummy food / with a lot of / . /

   ⬭   ▭   _____

9. I want / my / you to come / and visit / dream house / . /

   ⬭   ▭   _____

Revising Practice

Read the story and complete the tasks below.

Title: My Dream House

Ⓐ my dream house is a cottage by the sea.
It has eight bedrooms and three bathrooms.
1. A comfortable sofa is in the living room.
2. A bookshelf is in the study.
Ⓑ A big oven is in the kitchen◯
3. A table is in the dining room.
A nice tennis court is in the backyard.
A sports car and a bicycle are in the garage.
Ⓒ Dont you want to visit my dream house?

A. Correct sentences A, B, and C.

Ⓐ My dream house is a cottage by the sea.

Ⓑ _____

Ⓒ _____

B. Expand sentences 1, 2, and 3 with the given words.

1. **(with many cushions)**

   A comfortable sofa _____ is in the living room.

2. **(with many books)**

   A bookshelf _____ is in the study.

3. **(with six chairs)**

   A table _____ is in the dining room.

My Final Draft

Title:

<More Than 90 Words>

My Comment	☐ Good ☐ Excellent

Parent's Comment	☐ Good	☐ Excellent
Teacher's Comment	☐ Good	☐ Excellent

Sentence Practice

Put the words in order.

Subject + Verb + End of sentence

1. favorite / giraffe /is / My / animal / a / . /

   (My favorite animal) [is] _____ a giraffe. _____

2. they are / giraffes / I / like / because / so strong / . /

   (　　　) [　　　] _____

3. from the branches / can eat / of tall trees / leaves and fruit / They / . /

   (　　　) [　　　] _____

4. big eyes / and / long necks, / brown spots, / have / They / . /

   (　　　) [　　　] _____

5. so / they / I / are /giraffes / tall / like / because / . /

_____

6. strong, / Giraffes / tall, / are / and beautiful / . /

_____

7. scare away / can kick / their enemies / with their legs / They / . /

_____

and _____

8. so / they / because / are / I / beautiful / giraffes / like / . /

_____

9. amazing / Giraffes / are / animals / . /

_____

Revising Practice

Read the story and complete the tasks below.

Title: My Favorite Animal

My favorite animal is an eagle.

A I like eagles because they are amazing◯

1. They can fly in the sky.

I like eagles because they are so powerful.

B (they) can hunt with their pointed beaks.

I like eagles because they are so beautiful.

2. They have long wings and lovely feathers.

C Eagles are (amazing) powerful, and beautiful.

3. They are my favorite animals.

A. Correct sentences A, B, and C.

A _____

B _____

C _____

B. Expand sentences 1, 2, and 3 with the given words.

1. (very high)

They can fly _____ in the sky.

2. (sharp beaks)

They have _____, long wings, and lovely feathers.

3. (That's why)

_____ they are my favorite animals.

 My Final Draft

Title:

<More Than 100 Words>

🌱 Sentence Practice

Put the words in order.

Subject + Verb + End of sentence

1. is / an / My mom's / amazing / kitchen / place / . /

   (My mom's kitchen) [is] an amazing place.

2. turns / broccoli / She / into / delicious broccoli soup / . /

   (   ) [   ] _____

3. can / sweet / I / smell / pancakes / . /

   (   ) [   ] _____

4. has / and a / stove / huge oven / She / a fancy / . /

   (   ) [   ] _____

5. a / is / magic / It / box / like / . /

6. turns / She / sweet carrot cake / into / carrots / . /

7. apples / She / yummy apple pie / turns / into / . /

8. love / I / my mom / to help / in her special kitchen / . /

9. is / My / like / magician / mom / a / . /

Revising Practice

Read the story and complete the tasks below.

Title: Mom's Magic Kitchen

A My moms kitchen is a fun place.
1. It is like a magic land.
She has a gas stove and a great oven.
B she has shiny pans and large pots.
2. I can smell delicious bacon.
Every evening, I can smell tasty meat cooking.
3. My mom is like a magician.
She turns vegetables into yummy salad.
She turns eggs into delicious omelets.
C She turns oranges into fresh juice○
I love to watch her cook in her fabulous kitchen.

A. Correct sentences A, B, and C.

A _____

B _____

C _____

B. Expand sentences 1, 2, and 3 with the given words.

1. (great big)

It is like a _____ magic land.

2. (frying in a pan in the morning)

I can smell delicious bacon _____.

3. (when she cooks the most delicious food in the world)

My mom is like a magician _____

_____.

24 Unit 6 Mom's Magic Kitchen

My Final Draft

Title:

_____

_____

_____

_____

_____

_____

_____

_____

_____

_____

_____

_____

_____

_____

_____

_____

_____

<More Than 100 Words>

My Comment ☐ Good   ☐ Excellent

Parent's Comment ☐ Good ☐ Excellent
Teacher's Comment ☐ Good ☐ Excellent

How to Cook Hot Dogs

Language Sprouts

Sentence Practice

Put the words in order.

Subject	+	Verb	+	End of sentence

1. because / like / I / they / to / are / delicious / eat / and easy / hot dogs / to cook / . /

(I) [like] to eat hot dogs because they are delicious and easy to cook.

2. Heat / pot / water / of / a / . /

(X) [   ] _____

3. Add / onions, / some / ketchup, / and pickles / . /

(X) [   ] _____

4. on / a bun / Put / the sausages / one of / . /

(X) [   ] _____

5. Be / might get / careful / or you / burned / . /

6. are / the cooked / You / ready to enjoy / hot dog / . /

7. the sausages / Take out / from the pot / . /

8. the sausages / for about / Boil / five to six minutes / . /

9. need / sausages, / You / and some onions / hot dog buns, / . /

Read the story and complete the tasks below.

Title: How to Cook Hot Dogs

I like to eat hot dogs because they are delicious and easy to cook.

Ⓐ (there) are five steps to make a good hot dog.

1. First, put some sausages in a pot of water.

Second, boil the sausages for about five to six minutes.

Ⓑ Be careful, or (Y)ou might get burned.

2. Third, remove the sausages from the pot.

After that, put one of the sausages on a warm bun.

3. Finally, add some ketchup, onions, and pickles.

Ⓒ Now you are ready to enjoy the cooked hot dog ()

A. Correct sentences A, B, and C.

Ⓐ _____

Ⓑ _____

Ⓒ _____

B. Expand sentences 1, 2, and 3 with the given words.

1. (and put the pot on the stove)

First, put some sausages in a pot of water _____

_____ .

2. (and put them on a plate)

Third, remove the sausages from the pot _____

_____ .

3. (on the hot dog)

Finally, add some ketchup, onions, and pickles _____ .

Title:

<More Than 120 Words>

🌱 Sentence Practice

Put the words in order.

Subject + Verb + End of sentence

1. don't have to fly / to take pictures / People / to the sky / . /

   (People) [don't have to fly]   to the sky to take pictures.

2. like / flying robots / are / Drones / . /

   (   ) [   ] _____

3. can take / Drones / in the air / pictures and videos / . /

   (   ) [   ] _____

4. I / that / someday drones will be / believe / as important as cars / . /

   (   ) [   ] _____

5. can make / in many ways / safer / Drones / people / . /

6. people / can search for / who are lost / Drones / . /

7. can watch for / wildfires / Drones / and floods / . /

8. are / useful / Drones / and amazing / . /

9. can deliver / food / to people / Drones / or packages / . /

Revising Practice

Read the story and complete the tasks below.

Title: What Can Drones Do?

Drones are small flying machines.
Drones will change our world. They can do many things.
A First drones can take pictures and videos in the air.
1. Drones can take exciting videos for sports activities.
B Next, drones can sometimes make people safer
2. Drones can watch for wildfires or floods.
C last, drones can deliver things to people.
3. Drones can even deliver emergency supplies.
In the future, drones can change the way we work.

A. Correct sentences A, B, and C.

A _____

B _____

C _____

B. Expand sentences 1, 2, and 3 with the given words.

1. (so that people don't have to fly to the sky)

Drones can take exciting videos for sports activities _____

_____ .

2. (so that people can stay away from danger)

Drones can watch for wildfires or floods _____

_____ .

3. (so that people can be safe until they are rescued)

Drones can even deliver emergency supplies _____

_____ .

My Final Draft

Title:

What are robots, and what can they do? Robots are like humans.

<More Than 120 Words>

My Comment	☐ Good
	☐ Excellent

Parent's Comment	☐ Good	☐ Excellent
Teacher's Comment	☐ Good	☐ Excellent